To

_____

From

_____

Date

_____

Grandpa,
What Was It Like Growing Up Country?

Artwork by
DONALD ZOLAN

HARVEST HOUSE PUBLISHERS

EUGENE, OREGON

Grandpa, What Was It Like Growing Up Country?

Text Copyright © 2009 by Harvest House Publishers
Artwork Copyright © by Donald Zolan

Published by Harvest House Publishers
Eugene, Oregon 97402
www.harvesthousepublishers.com

"You Were a Country Boy" copyright © 2009 by Hope Lyda

ISBN 978-0-7369-2659-1

Design and production by Garborg Design Works, Savage, Minnesota

Scripture quotations are taken from the HOLY BIBLE, NEW INTERNATIONAL VERSION®. NIV®. Copyright©1973, 1978, 1984 by the International Bible Society. Used by permission of Zondervan. All rights reserved.

Printed in China

09 10 11 12 13 14 15 / LP / 10 9 8 7 6 5 4 3 2 1

You Were a Country Boy

On the day that you were born, Grandpa,
A new life began to unfold.
On the day that you were born,
A new story was about to be told.

I see you as a country boy
Hardworking, kind, and strong.
Full of curiosity and courage
And loving life all day long.

Did you raise horses and cows
And help out at harvesttime?
Did you get to drive a tractor
Or pluck fruit from the vine?

After you finished all your chores
Did you fish with friends at a favorite stream?
Did you skip rocks and explore new lands
And take quiet moments just to dream?

I can't wait to learn more and more
About the boy who turned out to be
The great and wonderful man
Who means so much to me.

On the day that I was born, Grandpa,
A new life began to unfold.
On the day that I was born,
Your story was ready to be told.

Grandpa_____,

tell me what it was like to grow up as a country boy.

With love,

_____

Your Story Begins

Grandpa, when is your birthday?

_____

Where were you born?

_____

What was going on in the world when you were little? _____

_____

_____

_____

_____

_____

_____

_____

_____

_____

How far you go in life depends on your being tender with the young, compassionate with the aged, sympathetic with the striving, and tolerant of the weak and the strong. Because some day in life you will have been all of these.

GEORGE WASHINGTON CARVER

What is one of your first memories? _____

_____

_____

_____

_____

_____

_____

_____

_____

_____

_____

_____

There is always one moment in childhood when the door opens and lets the future in.

GRAHAM GREENE

Our Family Tree

Grandpa, who were your parents? Grandparents? _____
_____
_____

Did you have any brothers or sisters? _____
_____
_____

What did you enjoy about being a part of your family?
_____
_____
_____
_____
_____
_____
_____
_____
_____
_____
_____
_____

For we are the same things our fathers have been;

We see the same sights our fathers have seen;

We drink the same stream, we feel the same sun,

And run the same course our fathers have run.

WILLIAM KNOX

Share with me a family story that was told to you as boy. _____

_____

_____

_____

_____

_____

_____

_____

_____

_____

_____

_____

Family Home

What was your childhood room like? Did you share it with siblings? _____

_____

_____

_____

_____

What town did you live in? _____

Did you have a big yard? _____

_____

_____

_____

How dear to this heart are the
scenes of my childhood,
When fond recollection recalls
them to view; the orchard,
the meadow, the deep-tangled
wildwood, and every loved spot,
which my infancy knew.

SAMUEL WOODWORTH

8

Describe your first home after you were married. _____
_____
_____
_____
_____
_____
_____

Grandpa, what is one of your favorite family memories? _____
_____
_____
_____
_____
_____
_____
_____
_____
_____
_____
_____

Starting Your Own Family

Grandpa, how did you meet Grandma? _____

_____

_____

_____

_____

_____

_____

When and where did you get married? _____

_____

What did you like most about your wedding? _____

_____

_____

_____

_____

_____

_____

_____

There shall be showers of blessing:
This is the promise of love.

DANIEL W. WHITTLE

There is nothing like a dream to create the future.

VICTOR HUGO

What were your deepest joys when you started your own family? _____

_____

_____

_____

_____

_____

What was my mom/dad like as a child?

_____

_____

_____

_____

_____

_____

_____

_____

_____

Traditions and Gatherings

Grandpa, what made your childhood family gatherings special? _____

_____

_____

_____

_____

_____

What activities did you enjoy during the holidays?

_____

_____

_____

_____

_____

_____

_____

_____

_____

Did you start new holiday traditions when you started a family? _____

_____

_____

_____

_____

_____

Share with me a tradition you hope I'll pass on to my kids some day. _____

_____

_____

_____

_____   The more we live, more brief appear
_____   Our life's succeeding stages:
_____   A day to childhood seems a year,
_____   And years like passing ages.
_____   The gladsome current of our youth,
_____   Ere passion yet disorders,
_____   Steals lingering like a river smooth
_____   Along its grassy borders.

Boyhood Memories

What is something special you have that belonged to your mother, father, or another relative?

_____

_____

_____

_____

_____

What memories of your parents, children, and life do you want to share with me?

_____

_____

_____

_____

_____

_____

_____

_____

_____

_____

_____

The closest friends I have made all through life have been people who also grew up close to a loved and loving grandfather and grandmother.

MARGARET MEAD

If you could share a "snapshot" of a special time
or place in your life, what would that image be of?

_____

_____

_____

_____

_____

_____

_____

When you picture my future, Grandpa, what do you hope it looks like?

_____

_____

_____

_____

_____

_____

_____

Free Time

When you had free time, what was the first thing you liked to do? _____

_____

_____

_____

_____

_____

Did you have a favorite book, game, or toy?

_____

_____

_____

_____

_____

_____

_____

_____

16

We don't stop playing because
we grow old; we grow old
because we stop playing.

GEORGE BERNARD SHAW

Which outdoor activities or sports did you like the most? _____

_____

_____

_____

_____

_____

What game would you love to play with me? _____

_____

_____

_____

_____

_____

_____

_____

_____

At the Kitchen Table

Describe what your family mealtime was like as a child. _____

_____

_____

_____

_____

_____

_____

_____

_____

For health and food,

For love and friends,

For everything Thy goodness sends,

Father in Heaven,

We thank Thee.

RALPH WALDO EMERSON

What was your favorite meal
for breakfast? lunch? dinner?

_____

_____

_____

_____

_____

_____

_____

The true harvest of my daily life
is somewhat as intangible and
indescribable as the tints of morning
or evening. It is a little stardust
caught, a segment of the rainbow
which I have clutched.

HENRY DAVID THOREAU

Did you have a favorite mealtime prayer or topic of conversation? _____

_____

_____

_____

_____

_____

_____

_____

_____

Country School

What was school like when you were a student? _____

_____

_____

_____

_____

_____

Which schools did you go to? _____

_____

_____

How did a teacher or a school experience influence your life? _____

_____

_____

_____

_____

_____

_____

_____

And though I now am small and young,

Of judgment weak and feeble tongue,

Yet all great, learned men, like me

Once learned to read their ABC.

DAVID EVERETT

What was your favorite subject? _____

_____

What kind of activities were you involved in throughout your school years?

_____

_____

_____

_____

_____

_____

_____

_____

_____

21

Helping Hands

As a kid, what chores were your responsibility? _____

_____

_____

_____

_____

_____

_____

_____

_____

_____

What was your favorite way of helping your mom or dad? _____

_____

_____

_____

_____

_____

_____

How did the country life teach you to help one another? _____

_____

_____

_____

What should I know about being a good helper? _____

_____

The LORD your God will bless you in all your
harvest and in all the work of your hands, and
your joy will be complete.

THE BOOK OF DEUTERONOMY

_____

_____

_____

Farm Friends

Grandpa, what pets did you have as a child?
What were their names?

_____

_____

_____

_____

_____

_____

Did you raise farm animals? Which kind?

_____

_____

_____

_____

_____

_____

_____

Which animals do you love the most? _____

_____

_____

What is your favorite story about a pet or animal? _____

_____

_____

_____

_____

My Pa held me up to the moo-cow-moo
So close I could almost touch:
An' I fed him a couple of times
Or two
An' I wasn't a 'fraid-cat much.

But, ef my Pa goes into the house
An' ef my Mama goes too,
I jest keep still like a little mouse
'Cause the moo-cow-moo might moo!

EDMUND VANCE COOKE

25

Growing Up Outdoors

What was the landscape like around your childhood home? _____

_____

_____

_____

_____

How did you enjoy nature? Did you climb trees, play hide-and-seek among the corn stalks, or fish at a nearby lake?

_____

_____

_____

_____

_____

_____

_____

_____

_____

_____

_____

If you could show me a special outdoor place from your childhood, what would it be?

_____

_____

_____

_____

_____

_____

> Oh! The old swimin' hole! In the long, lazy days
> When the humdrum of school made so many run-a-ways,
> How pleasant was the journey down the old dusty lane,
> Where the tracks of our bare feet was all printed so plain
> You could tell by the dent of the heel and the sole
> They was lots o' fun on hand at the old swimmin' hole.
>
> JAMES WHITCOMB RILEY

Why was it so meaningful to you? _____ .

_____

_____

_____

_____

_____

_____

_____

_____

_____

Best of Friends

Who were your friends when you were growing up? _____

_____

_____

_____

_____

_____

_____

What were your favorite activities to do with them? _____

_____

_____

_____

_____

_____

_____

But this I know, I love to play
Through meadow, among the hay;
Up the water and over the lea,
That's the way for Billy and me.
JAMES HOGG

How were you a good friend? _____

_____

_____

_____

_____

Grandpa, share a story about one of your special times with friends. _____

_____

_____

_____

_____

_____

_____

_____

_____

_____

_____

_____

What were some of the hard times your family experienced? _____

_____

_____

_____

_____

The life that counts must toil and fight;   _____

Must hate the wrong and love the right;   _____

Must stand for truth, by day, by night—   _____

This is the life that counts.   _____

AUTHOR UNKNOWN   _____

How did you and your family handle the tough days? _____

_____

_____

_____

_____

_____

_____

_____

Where does your courage come from, Grandpa? _____

_____

_____

_____

_____

_____

_____

What advice do you have for me when I am afraid or uncertain? _____

_____

_____

_____

_____

_____

_____

I believe in working when you work and in playing when you play and in giving and demanding a square deal in every act of life.

FROM THE *COUNTRY BOY'S CREED*

Country Faith

Did your family go to church? What was it like? _____

_____

_____

_____

_____

_____

_____

What values do people in the country hold dear? _____

_____

_____

_____

_____

_____

_____

_____

_____

_____

Our Creator would never have made such lovely days, and given us the deep hearts to enjoy them, above and beyond all thought, unless we were meant to be immortal.

NATHANIEL HAWTHORNE

What is your most treasured verse or memory from growing up with country faith?

_____

_____

_____

_____

_____

Grandpa, what is your hope and prayer for me?

_____

_____

_____

_____

_____

_____

_____

_____

Good Times

What or who made you laugh as a child? _____

_____

_____

_____

_____

_____

Do you remember a joke or funny song from your childhood? _____

_____

_____

_____

_____

_____

_____

_____

Among those whom I like or admire,
I can find no common denominator,
but among those whom I love, I can:
all of them make me laugh.

W.H. AUDEN

What was one of the best times you had with your family? _____

_____

_____

_____

_____

_____

_____

_____

_____   *The most wasted*
of all days is one
without laughter.
E.E. CUMMINGS

Share with me a story from your life that still makes you laugh. _____

_____

_____

_____

_____

_____

_____

_____

Big Dreams as a Small Boy

Grandpa, what did you daydream about as a boy? _____

_____

_____

_____

_____

What did you want to be when you grew up? _____

_____

_____

When you said your bedtime prayers, who and what did you pray for? _____

_____

_____

_____

_____

_____

_____

_____

_____

Today, what are the dreams you have for your life? _____

_____

_____

_____

_____

_____

What are your wishes for me, Grandpa?

_____

_____

_____

_____

_____

_____

_____

_____

He who gives a child a book,
Gives that child a sweeping look,
Through its pages
Down the ages.

Gives that child a ship to sail,
Where the far adventurers hail
Down the sea
Of destiny.

Gives that child great dreams to dream;
Sun-lit ways that glint and gleam
Where the sages
Tramp the ages.

WILLIAM STIDGER

37

Hobbies and Happiness

How did you express your creativity when you were young? _____

_____

_____

_____

_____

_____

Did your father or someone teach you a craft or a hobby that you enjoyed?

_____

_____

_____

_____

_____

_____

_____

Grandpa, did you collect anything as a boy? Do you collect anything now? _____

_____

_____

_____

_____

What would you like to teach me to do? _____

_____

_____

_____

_____

_____

_____

_____

_____

Sweet childish days, that were as long
As twenty days are now.

WILLIAM WORDSWORTH

39

Being Neighborly

What was the town or community like that you grew up in? _____

_____

_____

_____

_____

_____

_____

_____

_____

_____

Did you participate in your town's celebrations, parades, or the county fair? _____

_____

_____

_____

_____

_____

_____

_____

Along the street there comes
A blare of bugles, a ruffle of drums;
And loyal hearts are beating high:
Hats off!
The flag is passing by!

HENRY HOLCOMB BENNETT

Tell me a story about growing up in a country town. _____

_____

_____

_____

_____

_____

How can I be a good neighbor to people in my life? _____

_____

_____

_____

_____

_____

The Gift of Being a Grandpa

Grandpa, where were you when you found out that my story had begun?

_____

_____

_____

_____

_____

_____

Describe one of the most surprising joys of being a grandparent? _____

_____

_____

_____

_____

_____

_____

_____

_____

_____

_____

_____

42

What do you want me to know about life? _____

_____

_____

_____

_____

_____

_____

What do you want me to know about you? _____

_____

_____

_____

_____

_____

_____

_____

_____

_____

_____

> You will find as you look back upon life
> that the moments when you have really
> lived are the moments when you have
> done things in the spirit of love.
>
> HENRY DRUMMOND

43

The Harvest of Country Life

How was country living different then compared to life now? _____

_____

_____

_____

_____

_____

_____

What is the most important lesson you
learned from growing up country?

_____

_____

_____

_____

_____

_____

_____

We could never have loved the earth so well
if we had had no childhood in it.

GEORGE ELIOT

Tell me all about your favorite aspects of country living. _____

_____

_____

_____

_____

_____

_____

What do you hope I experience that was a part of your childhood? _____

_____

_____

_____

_____

_____

_____

_____

A Letter from Grandpa

_____

_____

_____

_____

_____

_____

_____

_____

_____

_____

_____

_____

Every man's memory is his private literature.

ALDOUS HUXLEY

Grandpa, what would you want me to know most of all? _____

_____

_____

_____

_____

_____

_____

_____

_____

_____

_____

_____

_____

_____

_____

I share these memories with my dear grandchild:

_____

Love,

_____

My grandfather always taught us that the first step of
wisdom is silence, and the second step is listening.

ARNOLD BETTERMAN

48